For Laurie
A wonderful maker of things

My thanks to Jazzy Laurie Tom Sarah Stevie
Ollie Rufus Ben Jill

First published 2012 by Walker Books Ltd
87 Vauxhall Walk, London SE11 5HJ

This edition published 2015

2 4 6 8 10 9 7 5 3 1

© 1990 – 2015 Lucy Cousins
Lucy Cousins font © 1990 – 2015 Lucy Cousins
The moral rights of the author/illustrator have been asserted.

Maisy™. Maisy is a trademark of Walker Books Ltd, London.

Printed in China

British Library Cataloguing in Publication Data:
a catalogue record for this book is available from the British Library.

ISBN 978-1-4063-5797-4

www.walker.co.uk

This Walker book belongs to:

....

....

....

Make with Maisy

by Lucy Cousins

WALKER BOOKS

AND SUBSIDIARIES

LONDON · BOSTON · SYDNEY · AUCKLAND

A message for the grown-ups

Making things is fun.

Maisy makes lots of things in this book that I hope you and your children will enjoy making too. The instructions are very simple, and you don't need to follow them if you have your own ideas. I hope that you will already have most of the things needed in your home, but if not, just use something different.

While your children are enjoying making things, please make sure they are safe. Help them where necessary and always use:

• PVA glue and glue sticks which are washable and non-toxic

• child-friendly scissors with rounded ends

• washable non-toxic paints, like poster paints

Any birthdays coming up? I think homemade gifts are the best presents. I still cherish things my teenage children made for me when they were little.

Have fun!

Love,

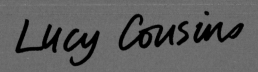

Maisy loves making things.

These are some of the things she uses.

You can make things too.

Beady butterfly

flitter

flutter

Maisy uses

card

scissors

paints and brushes

pipe cleaners

sticky tape

beads

How to make it

1. Cut a butterfly body from the card and paint it in stripy colours.

2. Thread beads onto two pipe cleaners.

3. Bend the pipe cleaners into wing shapes. Twist the ends and tape them to the back of the body.

4. For the antennae, bend a pipe cleaner in half and tape it to the butterfly's head.

5. Thread on two beady eyes and curl the ends.

Box house

Maisy uses

shoe box

piece of card

scissors

sticky tape

paints and brushes

Maisy has made a house for Panda too.

How to make it

1. On the bottom of a box, draw a door.

2. Get a grown-up to help you cut out the door. Do not cut one of the long sides, that way the door can swing open.

3. For the roof, fold a piece of card lengthways. Stand the house upright and stick the roof on top with tape.

4. Add a card chimney and paint and decorate your house!

Blossom tree

Maisy uses

large piece of card

paints and brushes

drinking straw

tissue paper

glue stick

How to make it

1. Paint a large tree on the card, with four main branches.

2. Add water to paint; brush watery paint drops onto the main branches.

3. Using the straw, blow the paint in different directions – making lots of little branches.

4. Scrunch balls of blossom from torn pieces of tissue paper.

5. When the painted tree is dry, stick on the tissue blossoms.

cheep cheep

Food picture

Maisy uses

paper

PVA glue and brush

*beans, spices, seeds,
dried herbs and tea leaves*

How to make it

1. Paint a flower face with glue on a sheet
of paper and sprinkle some seeds on it.

2. Gently shake the loose seeds off.

3. Create petals, leaves and stalks; glue, stick and shake
one at a time until you have a beautiful garden!

Vegetable print

Maisy uses

vegetables and fruit

paper towel

paper plates

paints

paper

How to make it

1. Ask a grown-up to help you cut up some fruit and vegetables. Pat the slices dry with a paper towel.

2. Spread paint onto paper plates.

3. Dip the food into the paint and print patterns on the paper.

Maisy uses it as wrapping paper.

Useful pot

maisy
recycles pictures
of her
favourite animals.

Maisy uses

*plastic pot from
her recycling box*

PVA glue and brush

*pictures cut out from
magazines*

stickers

ribbon

How to make it

1. Find a plastic pot.

2. Use glue and a brush to stick on pictures and ribbon.

3. Add stickers.

Maisy keeps pencils in her useful pot.

Painted pebbles

Maisy uses

pebbles

paints and brushes

PVA glue

How to make them

1. Find some pebbles that are nice shapes and colours.

2. Paint them with bright pictures and patterns.

3. If you want to keep your pebbles outside, paint them with PVA glue to make them waterproof.

Feather mask

Maisy uses

paper plate

scissors

paints and brushes

feathers

sticky tape

lollipop stick

How to make it

1. Hold the plate to your face and draw eye holes.

2. Ask a grown-up to help you cut out the eye holes.

3. Paint a colourful face on the plate.

4. Use sticky tape to fix feathers to the back.

5. For a handle, tape the lollipop stick to the bottom of the mask.

Is that you, Cyril?

Paper lanterns

Maisy uses

coloured paper

paints and brushes

scissors

sticky tape

ribbon or string

How to make them

1. Cut some rectangles of paper and paint patterns on them. Leave to dry.

2. Fold the paper in half, lengthways.

3. Make a row of cuts along the folded edge.

4. Open out the paper. Roll it so the short ends meet. Join with sticky tape.

5. For a handle, cut a strip of paper and stick it on the lantern.

6. Make more lanterns.

7. Thread ribbon or string through the handles and hang them up.

Maisy is going to have a party.

Tissue flowers

buzzzzz

Maisy makes flowers for Ella.

Maisy uses

tissue paper

scissors

pipe cleaners

beads

How to make them

1. To make one flower, hold together several layers of tissue paper and roughly cut a circle.

2. Pierce the centre of the tissue circles with a pipe cleaner and drop a bead on top.

3. Bend the pipe cleaner around the bead and twist.

4. Scrunch up the tissue circles then separate the petals.

5. Make more flowers. If you want to make them sparkly, dab with glue and add glitter.

Vegetable animals

Maisy uses

fruit and vegetables

cocktail sticks

cutting board and knife

How to make them

1. What fruit and vegetables will you use?

2. What friends will you make?

3. Ask a grown-up to help if you need to cut things up. Use the cocktail sticks to join things together (snap the sticks for smaller pieces).

Hello, Courgette Dog.

Charlie likes Mr Aubergine.

Button bowl

Maisy uses

air dry clay (which can be bought online or from a craft shop)

buttons, beads, sequins, shells and glitter

How to make it

1. Squeeze the clay in your hands and make a ball.

2. Press your thumbs into the middle and use your fingers to shape a bowl.

3. Flatten out the bottom to make a base.

4. Press buttons and other decorations into the clay.

5. Leave clay to dry for about 24 hours.

Panda loves the button bowl.

Pasta Necklace

Maisy uses

dry pasta tubes

brushes and paints

ball of string

scissors

PVA glue

sequins

How to make it

1. Paint some pasta tubes in different colours and leave to dry.

2. Thread the tubes onto a ball of string.

3. Measure to check the necklace will fit over your head.

4. Cut the string and tie a knot.

5. Glue on sequins for extra sparkle.

It's so pretty, maisy!

twinkly

sparkly

shiny

lovely

Sparkly Crown

Maisy uses

coloured or painted card

shiny wrappers,
foil and stickers

sticky tape

glue stick

How to make it

1. Measure the card around your head and cut to size.

2. Cut a zigzag around the top.

3. Using the glue stick, decorate your crown
with shiny wrappers, foil and stickers.

4. Join the ends with sticky tape.

Hello,
King Eddie!

Magic Wax painting

Maisy uses

white paper

white wax crayon or candle

paints and brushes

How to make it

1. Draw a picture with the wax crayon.

2. Brush watery paint over and around the wax lines. Watch your picture appear.

Rainbow tiger

Maisy uses

clean sheet of paper

lots of things from her recycling box

PVA glue

brushes and paints

How to make it

1. Lay down a sheet of paper.

2. Cut the tiger's body from cardboard and stick it to the paper.

3. Create the rest of the tiger by sticking down recycled things.

Brilliant biscuits

Maisy uses

plain biscuits

icing sugar

sweets and sprinkles

writing icing

fruit

bowl and spoons

How to make them

1. Wash your hands.

2. Put 4 heaped tablespoons of icing sugar into a bowl.

3. Add 3-4 teaspoons of water and stir.

4. Spread the icing over the biscuits and leave to dry a little.

5. Decorate with sprinkles, sweets, writing icing and fruit.

Yummy!

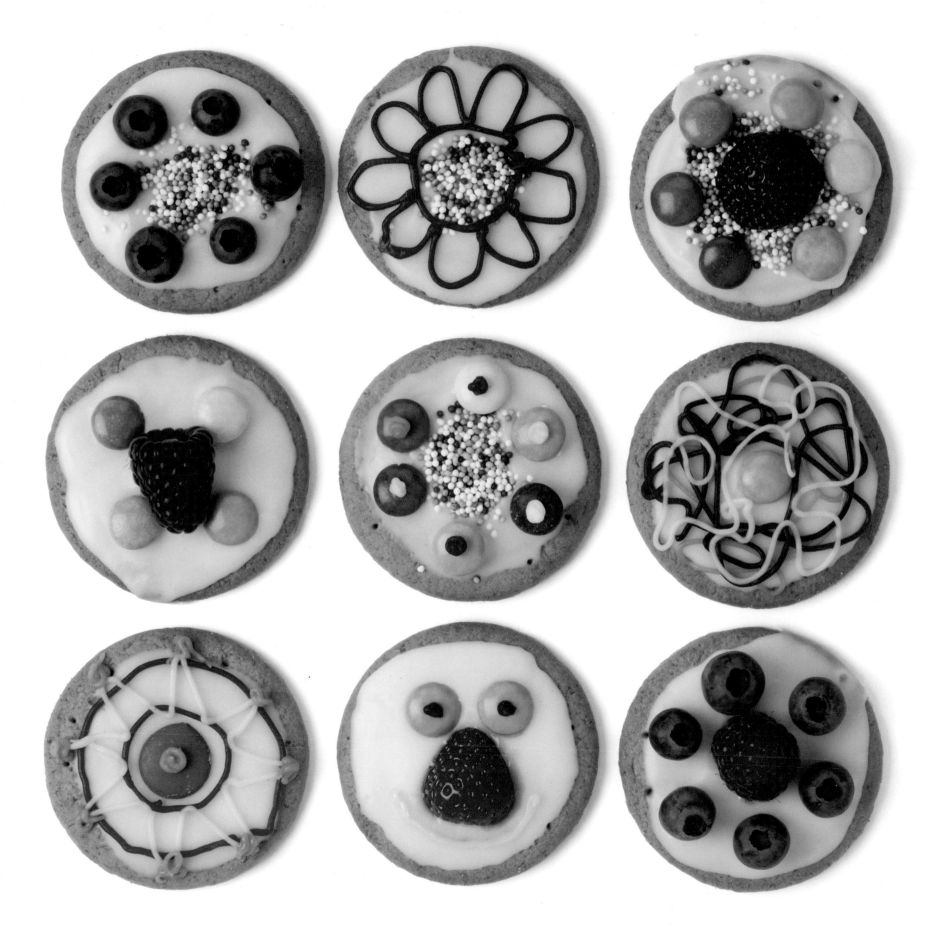

Maisy has been very busy.
She has made lots of things.

Well done, Maisy.

Lucy Cousins

is the multi-award-winning creator of much-loved character Maisy.
She has written and illustrated over 100 books and has sold
over 26 million copies worldwide.

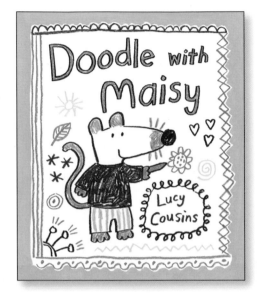

978-1-4063-4499-8

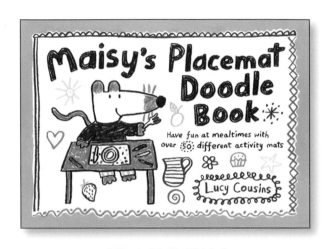

978-1-4063-5299-3

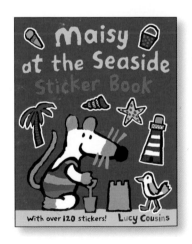

978-1-4063-5858-2

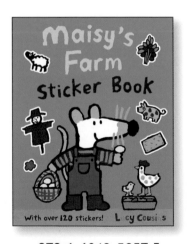

978-1-4063-5857-5

978-1-4063-5400-3

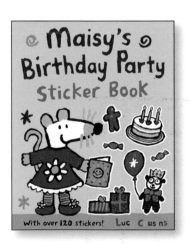

978-1-4063-5640-3

Available from all good booksellers

www.walker.co.uk